BENINGFIELD'S
—— ENGLISH VILLAGES ——

GORDON BENINGFIELD

VIKING

Published in the United Kingdom Exclusively for

This edition published 2004 by Selectabook Ltd

SELECTABOOK
Folly Road
Roundway
Devizes
Wiltshire SN10 2HT

Produced by TAJ BOOKS
27 Ferndown Gardens
Cobham
Surrey
KT11 2BH
United Kingdom

Email : info@tajbooks.com

First published 1983

Printed and bound in China

ISBN 1-84406-021-7

CONTENTS

INTRODUCTION

I have always loved villages and have spent most of my life living in them. True village life is valuable and precious – so its conservation is essential. A rural landscape, with its farms, fields and wildlife, needs villages – practical ones made of local materials suiting the people and their occupations. From my earliest days, architecture was important to me; I was interested in the school and the church as well as the house where we lived. I left school at fifteen and went to work in ecclesiastical art, which involved architecture too.

When travelling to different parts of the country, you should be able to have some idea of where you are without looking at road signs and maps, because the architecture of the villages should reflect the character of their area. What concerns me these days is that you can travel far and wide, yet the village where your journey ends could be anywhere; in terms of architectural design and materials the result can be pitiful. Often with nationwide builders, the end product looks the same, from John o'Groat's to Land's End. Some local builders are not much better – what they build just seems to depend on what they have in the yard at the time, so you lose both quality and character.

We want to see a landscape with the individual architecture and character that belong to it. One place where this can be found is the Cotswolds. The Cotswolds really are lovely and the area deserves praise and recognition. Character and quality have been maintained – and they could be maintained elsewhere too. If you go to Kent or Dorset or anywhere else, you should be able to experience the joy and pleasure of architecture which is part of the local rural landscape.

Sadly, traditional village life has become as endangered as the dormouse and the skylark. The car and commuting have been a disaster for villages – bringing urbanization to the countryside. The charm of a cottage lies in its texture, its colour and the way it fits almost naturally into its immediate surroundings – but today's country cottage is being bought by outsiders and tarted up so that it becomes out of sympathy with its surroundings. Then the garden is ruined, and a nice little hedge is pulled up and replaced with a brick wall, a couple of concrete lions and a gate. Everyone seems to want to be Lord of the Manor now, with gravel instead of lawns and gardens. This urbanization of the countryside deeply disturbs me. The people often don't fit in either. They don't become involved with village life, not even getting to know their neighbours. They don't join the church or the Women's Institute, and they treat the village as a glorified bed-and-breakfast area. I look upon the loss of the village, in all its shapes and forms, with just as much concern as I feel for the change and loss of landscape or wildlife. So I decided to write this celebration of the traditional English village.

I felt that for this book it would be good to travel around as many counties as time would allow, to search out special places, with marvellous architecture and country characters, where village life and the village scene still go hand in hand. The search was worth it, for there are many beautiful areas remaining in Britain – stunning landscapes with beautiful buildings – still with the people to go with them, the craftsmen and the ordinary villagers, even if they are becoming harder to find with each passing year.

My village upbringing was extremely important to me. I arrived in Hertfordshire in 1941 as a four-year-old, and the influence was so great, even at that age, that it has never left me. We were surrounded by farms, and the village school was so vital that even now a group of us meet up once a month. The friends I have known since I was five, when the war was on, remain great chums and we still do many things together. It is an example of the benefits of small communities – I lived and went to school in the same village, so that fifty-five years on the friendships are still there. Small is not only beautiful, it is also good. The broader and bigger a community becomes, the more divorced it is from village life – the people become separated from its quality and character.

I have had some great journeys and seen some delightful villages, people, little shops and large windmills. It has been enormously interesting, particularly the architecture. But there have been other things to paint than buildings, like the marvellous apples at Brogdale, the national collection of 2,000 apple trees. I was in Kent looking for oast-houses, when I found myself near Faversham, driving past Brogdale when all the blossom was out. I had to stop and get totally lost in apples that day. The orchards were lovely and, of course, at one time most villages had their old apple trees and orchards. Even the acre around my cottage has evidence of the old apple trees that were planted, so apples, like roses, are very much connected with villages. All my journeys were exciting and I came across things quite by chance that I would never have imagined. One day I was driving in the Cotswolds, went to look at a church spire and found a thatched cricket pavilion, on saddle-stones nearby. A cricket match was being played on a pitch that was still ridge and furrow – I couldn't believe it. I hope this book conveys the joy and pleasure that can still be found in England – search it out yourselves before it is too late.

HERTFORDSHIRE

My village journeys began with me walking out of my cottage garden. Just coming round from the front door, through the rose arch, you can see part of the sixteenth-century cottage. I love the idea of a gate – in a field, in

a hedge, or in a cottage garden: when you just see a bit of sunlight beyond, it makes you want to go through and explore. I also like simple things, such as my orchard in February with its carpet of snowdrops. I am no gardener, although I do like to have a garden with wildness all around it.

13

Although I have lived here for twenty-one years, I haven't really painted a great deal locally. The Parish of Great Gaddesden is sprawling and has two bridges over the River Gade. I live at Water End, which is one of the hamlets

within the parish and close to one of the bridges. The river is still quite a pleasant chalk stream full of trout, which Chamberlain and Churchill fished for before the war. It also has kingfishers, yellow iris, and various waterfowl.

In the winter, snipe and woodcock visit. There is much cover deliberately left on the banks for mammals, insects and birds — a chalk stream has more than just fish. The 2,000 acres of the Gaddesden estate dominate the parish, with 4,000 acres of National Trust land behind it. Looking down from the top of the park, you get a good view of the village of Great Gaddesden with its church and trees. It's a windy spot, but I think it creates quite a warm feeling on the edge of the Chiltern Hills. Even though it is close to Hemel Hempstead, you can still step out into the English countryside.

Most of the houses in Water End are Grade II listed buildings; they are usually timber-framed. It is also designated an Area of Outstanding Natural Beauty and some parts are conservation areas as well.

WATER END

When I think of Great Gaddesden, I also think of Ashridge. At the base of the ridge there is a picturesque village called Aldbury. One of the paintings looks down to part of the village from the side of the downland. Then I've shown its most famous area where there is still a whipping post and stocks; behind them is an attractive timber-framed property and the village pond.

Although Aldbury receives many visitors, it has retained its charm and atmosphere. It still has its shop too. It is safeguarded by its proximity to Ashridge and the National Trust. Westmill is another of Hertfordshire's delightful villages, retaining so much character.

16

WESTMILL

Gordon Beningfield

BUCKINGHAMSHIRE

Of the following pictures of places in Buckinghamshire, there are three here from the village of Hambleden. A fourth, of the lych-gate, looking towards the church and with a cottage on the left, appears as the frontispiece.

The village shop with the pump in front of it is charming. It has little notices on the fence advertising goods and services. It is a paper shop and general store. The MG just happened to be there (I put it in simply because I love MGs and have two earlier models myself, but it really was there).

The drawing that I couldn't resist doing was of this lovely little garage. It looks as if it is still the 1930s; even the modern petrol pump is tucked away. The best thing about the garage at Hambleden is that, although its wares are modern, it still fits in with the village scene. Today, garages can be some of the ugliest constructions you can imagine – Lego architecture – you can hardly call them buildings. They are made with the cheapest possible materials, then the owners invariably start hanging out flags, bunting and their special offers. It is all completely unnecessary. Surely there is no reason why a garage can't be in sympathy with its surroundings, reflecting the character and architecture of a village. I do think there should be very strong planning controls on garages. So, I was

attracted to this tiny construction because it has hardly been altered and looks in keeping with the rest of the architecture.

Walking through the village, I couldn't believe my eyes when I looked across a garden full of vegetables and flowers. It was so marvellous to see the washing hanging out – as all washing should – blowing in the summer breeze. Again, it was something I stumbled across. It reminded me of H. E. Bates and his delightful story about Uncle Silas – one of my favourite books.

HAMBLEDEN

Here I found a hazy warm summer atmosphere; the whole thing was a riot of colour, as lovely country gardens should be. It typified for me the quality and character of a village garden. There were no brick walls, patios or barbecues. It was a jumble of typical English flowers and vegetables. Even the garden paths were just packed down with cinders or earth. It was charming and pure Uncle Silas. I'm so glad to hear that there is soon going to be a television production of *My Uncle Silas*. It will give pleasure to millions, just like *The Darling Buds of May*, and if I was choosing the location this would be it.

Beyond the town of Aylesbury I came across two villages, one slightly larger than the other, called Brill and Quainton. Both have windmills and there is also a restored steam railway at Quainton. There are rather a lot of windmills in this book; it was not planned, they simply cropped up and they are charming. Both these mills have been restored and are very quaint, as you can see in the pencil drawing. The mill at Quainton is unusually tall and dominates the scene. You can see it across the landscape; in the general view over the meadows, it stands high above the village. To do the pencil drawing, I went down into the village, looking up across the village green. It is a lovely area of Buckinghamshire – just on the edge of the Chilterns.

From Quainton I wandered on a bit further and came to Brill. It is quite high, and from the common where the windmill sits you can see for miles across the landscape. I was excited to find two large badger setts not far from the common. I painted the scene with the mill dominating. It was very green the first time I visited, but when I returned on another day there was this marvellous pinkish sky. The pink of the sky reflected on to the common and

slightly changed the tone, which particularly appealed to me. Although I am concentrating on the village theme for this book, I haven't stuck rigidly to it and have included a tree, a bird, a person laying a hedge and even Father Christmas in a barn with reindeer. At Brill it was this interesting light that made me want to paint the picture.

The other drawing is of the windmill at Brill. I walked around the common and along the lanes looking at the different angles and possibilities. After doing a considerable amount of work on the original water-colour, I suddenly saw this view through the boughs of an oak tree. It was so attractive and pleasant that I did a pencil drawing of it as well. I love its texture and shape.

QUAINTON

25

Windmills are always interesting. They have stood for so long that they have become a real part of the rural landscape. In terms of conservation, they provide natural energy, which we are still experimenting with even today. The people of the past were more in tune with the natural world, and wind was an

energy source they recognized and appreciated – today we seem to have gone in a different direction. When looking at a windmill purely as a subject to paint and draw, you have to try to include the feeling of natural energy that a windmill creates. Of course, those who designed and erected the windmills were thinking not of pretty pictures, but of a piece of functional architecture.

BRILL

26

gordon heueuigfield,

THE COTSWOLDS

Only an hour and a half away from home and I am in the Cotswolds, at Burford. The authorities in the Cotswolds have achieved a great deal: in response to pressure from the public, they have maintained the most beautiful architecture you could possibly find. They have been very strict in the way that ordinary people and businesses have been allowed to improve their properties; other areas should follow their example. They have really looked after the architecture and quality of their villages.

Burford, with its great wide street, feels exciting from the moment you arrive. It has charming shops, with no supermarkets, and then, down at the bottom and over the bridge, there is the Windrush. It is a lovely river, which I first saw on a works outing back in the early 1960s when I was still involved in ecclesiastical art. I remember leaning over the bridge with other sculptors and painters; we were watching a mayfly on the surface of the water. More recently, when I was leaning over the bridge, I was tempted to walk out into the water meadows. I turned round and saw the spire of the church; it was all so marvellous, especially the light – it is the light that dominates and dictates landscape painting. The sky was dark, but shafts of rather sharp light cut across the landscape; then there was the river and all those buttercups – I couldn't resist it. It was the start of a perfect day, and so I painted the scene.

LOWER

SLAUGHTER

Leaving Burford, I arrived at Little Barrington. There the cottages are of honey-coloured stone, and one or two of them have interesting doorways. The village is surrounded by a green that was once a quarry; it is a very tranquil scene, with the village nestling into its hollow.

I wanted to paint the Slaughters, which, like many Cotswold villages, are very special for me. My father took me to the cinema in St Albans in 1944 to see a film called *The Tawny Pipit*, with Sir Bernard Miles in the part of the old Colonel. It was mainly about a bird that laid its eggs in a field, then suffered the pressures faced by today's wildlife, such as people stealing the eggs, the Army doing tank manoeuvres and so on. It was a charming and simple film and, because of the bird, the nest, the eggs, and the Hardyesque

BURFORD

LITTLE

BARRINGTON

31

Gordon Beningfield.

landscape, which was almost dreamlike, I never forgot it. Then, only six or seven years ago, I discovered in a copy of the *Countryman* an article about the production of this film, which said that it had been made in Upper and Lower Slaughter. So I went there for a long weekend with my wife, Betty, and my school chums, and it was just wonderful. I had to paint it.

The only difference between then and now is that it is not quite so rustic. There are lots of lawn-mowers and mechanical implements available these days, so that places do seem to be more 'gardened'. But there is still a great charm and atmosphere about Upper and Lower Slaughter.

UPPER

SLAUGHTER

LOWER

SLAUGHTER

In the film, the roadside verges were hardly cut because it was wartime; I do not understand why so many verges have to be cut these days – it makes everywhere too tidy and suburban. Unfortunately, this fashion seems to have spread everywhere. However, despite this, there is still a delightful atmosphere at the Slaughters and I enjoyed going back there. The water-mill looks almost as it did in the film. You can stroll from it across the meadows to Upper Slaughter and it is absolutely charming.

In addition to its great charm, Upper Slaughter is still very rural. The amazing thing is that the architecture depicted in *The Tawny Pipit* is still there. I also found the tree – just above the stream that runs through the centre of Upper Slaughter – that appears in a sequence towards the end of the film where the villagers assemble beneath its branches. I was glad to find it still standing today. It dominates my painting as a major part of the composition – just beyond the tiny, low bridge that spans that small stretch of water.

There are many lovely places in the Cotswolds that I remember from years ago, and I was tempted to stay and paint more. I had painted a picture at Wyck Rissington for someone there twenty years ago; I vaguely remembered being there and painting a picture of stoats. While I was wandering the lanes, a tiny green opened up and there was a cottage, which I recognized immediately. I saw a man standing by the cottage; it was the same person I had painted the picture for twenty years earlier. So we had a cup of tea and it was lovely to see him and the picture again. It was a wonderful accident. Sometimes, I think, you find more exciting things by chance than by planning.

LOWER

SLAUGHTER

Stanway gave me another example of the joys of unplanned wandering. I thought I would just look down into a little valley which seemed interesting. It was very small, but at the bottom I discovered a cricket match in progress. They were playing on an old field of ridge and furrow, although the wicket had been flattened out a bit. Despite the bumpy outfield, it had the most superb pavilion. It was thatched, made of wood, and stood on saddle-stones.

There were people on the veranda and bikes leaning against it — it was so typically English, it was wonderful. When I got home I was reading about villages and, quite by chance, I discovered a paragraph about the ground and its thatched pavilion. Apparently, it was donated by J. M. Barrie — the author of *Peter Pan*. I've had similar experiences with Turner and Hardy: I have been thinking about them and have then come across things associated with them, almost as if I had been directed that way. Before leaving this idyllic scene, I should explain that saddle-stones were used in the old days. They supported straw stacks to prevent the straw from getting damp.

STANWAY

Gordon Beningfield

ESSEX

After the Cotswolds I wandered off into Essex. You can spend a lifetime finding subjects to paint and enjoy and, once again, I was not disappointed. During the short trip to Finchingfield I passed along a country lane on a lovely, warm summer day. There, by a well-restored thatched farmhouse, with big thatched barns, was a perfect cart shed standing by three trees. It was well maintained and, astonishingly, it had a cart tucked low under its thatched roof. It was all so sensible — carts need fresh air and a breeze to keep them dry, but the roof was low enough to stop the rain getting in. I hadn't seen one as interesting as this before; it must have been quite an early one. It made such an impression that I painted a water-colour of it. I remember the sun on that day — it was dazzling me, being beyond the shed, which made it very difficult to paint.

Then I travelled on to Finchingfield, which is a fascinating place. There, beyond an open pond, I found yet another windmill. As I wandered round to look at it, I passed a charming farmhouse. By its gate was a rose arch covered with a beautiful, pale, old English rose, standing side by side with hollyhocks. If you looked through the arch itself, you could see the entrance of the farmhouse. It was a combination that summed up summer in an English village. It was

NEAR

FINCHINGFIELD

41

more than just the roses round the door – although they somehow seemed to epitomize the whole subject.

I love gardens that mingle with the wild wherever possible, and old roses are perfect for this – they are irresistible, particularly the traditional varieties. The Alexander rose is so simple and that is the one shown here in a whole-page close-up – it adds a nice blaze of colour. They are so much like the wild rose, maybe a bit more robust in colour and size, and what I would expect to see in a country village.

It is wonderful just roaming around – looking, watching and listening – to see what happens. It is very seldom that I return after a day out without subjects that I want to paint.

FINCHINGFIELD

43

FINCHINGFIELD

44

CAMBRIDGESHIRE

My travels to Cambridgeshire are very frequent because of the connection I have with Bird's Farm in the village of Barton and my old friend Robin Page. I interviewed him in 1978 for a television programme called *In the Country*, and we have been friends ever since. I am also a Trustee of the Countryside Restoration Trust, which Robin set up in 1993 and of which he is Chairman, and so I visit Barton once a month for meetings. The CRT is an extremely exciting and highly successful conservation group, although it has only been going for three years. The idea is to farm in a sensitive but profitable way, while maintaining, enhancing and considering landscape, as well as creating habitats for wildlife. When we buy our first farm, the CRT will naturally consider the architecture too. There will be important buildings to maintain, or maybe even to create, and we will be extremely sympathetic to the immediate surroundings.

Ray ('Badger') Walker is on the CRT management committee and, although he is by profession a computer engineer, he is also an expert hedge-layer, working on the farm and on the Trust land in his spare time. So I decided to do a painting of Badger in action, starting to lay a hedge. The field is close to an area where we are creating barn owl habitat by leaving rough areas in the meanders of the brook for small mammals – owl food. Not

every hedge needs to be laid: some can be left full and rich to bear fruit for over-wintering birds and mammals.

Certainly, by a road, even if you are hedge-laying, it is best to leave it as high as possible. This then forces the barn owls upwards and over the road safely. Thousands of barn owls get killed on our roads each year – a tragedy. Here I have shown Badger in action, and in the background is Robin Page, burning the trimmings. That is the other good thing about hedge-laying, the trimmings are burnt while the big wood is kept for logs – ideal for an open fireplace in winter. At times the fire almost went out and Robin had to jump up and down on it to make it burn – luckily he survived injury.

Later on in the year I returned to a newly created hay meadow, along a nearby hedge, sponsored by the Country Gentlemen's Association. Close by there is an attractive, simple footbridge going over the brook, constructed by Robin's brother, John. In the foreground are cowslips and then just beyond is a stile. I have painted it in a romantic way, as I always love the idea of disappearing through a hole in a hedge, over a small bridge like this one, or over a stile, and melting into the landscape. That is the way the country should be treated – with great respect, appreciation and reverence. So I feel that the subject, simple as it may be, just captured the gentle quality of the English countryside at this time in the spring.

During the year, Badger found himself an adoptive son. Travelling home late one night, he saw a dead sow badger on the side of the road with a very young cub at its side. It was so young that it shouldn't really have been above ground. Why it was there is a mystery, but it was still alive – just. Badger

rescued it and reared it. While he was laying the hedge he would down tools every hour to check up on, and feed, Billy Badger, who became a large, robust animal. He has since been handed over to a wildlife refuge in Leicestershire, where he has a big compound and is very happy. By the way, the reason Ray Walker is known as 'Badger' Walker is because of his fixation on badgers; it made his year to find this black-and-white striped baby.

BARTON

48

I enjoy my visits to Barton, as the CRT is interested in encouraging village life and traditions all through the seasons. At the end of the year, Father Christmas now comes to Bird's Farm with his reindeer. It is a remarkable evening. Last year there were excited children queuing up to enter the lamplight of the cow shed. Their faces shone and their eyes sparkled when they saw the reindeer standing in the straw. One of Rudolph's friends was an attractive white deer. The famous animals come from Britain's only herd of free-ranging reindeer, in the Cairngorms. Each year they are brought south, a month before Christmas, by the herders and owners, Alan and Tilly Smith. They are marvellous people, interesting and knowledgeable, and they really love their deer. Father Christmas was there too, answering to the name of Ken, our Trust Treasurer. I nearly let the cat out of the bag, as I kept calling him Ken instead of Father Christmas. It will not happen again, as I call him Father Christmas all the time now, even at our Trust meetings, just to be on the safe side. It was a tremendous evening – happy and lovely to be part of. It is incredible really, to go to a small village in Cambridgeshire and find Father Christmas in an eighteenth-century timber-framed barn; the whole image was wonderful. It couldn't have been more perfect; not only did the children find it exciting, but the parents enjoyed it too.

NORFOLK

I remember heading to Norfolk from Waresley in Cambridgeshire. I am a bad navigator and never know where I am. I ended up in rather a nice village where a woman was standing outside a delightful cottage. After showing some surprise that I had no idea where I was, she told me that I was in Old Hunstanton. It was an attractive little place, although rather cold in early December, and what interested me was the construction of the cottages. They had Norfolk tiles on the roof, but the walls appeared to be made of an amazing sort of orange porridge. The texture and the construction were fascinating. It will be interesting to see if our present whizz-kid architects, with their umpteen A levels, will be able to construct buildings that retain their character and craftsmanship for years on end like these cottages have.

I drew a study sheet. The one at the bottom is a simple church at Stow Bardolph. I was only passing by, but I have a weakness for churches and stopped to do this little sketch. It is nothing more than the combination of two trees and the church in the middle. It was a small village and that was the scene at the centre – it just appealed to me.

I then arrived, quite unplanned, at Cley, and yes, there was another windmill. Travelling along the road, I didn't even see the mill at first. Suddenly there it was – part of the landscape of a Norfolk village that I felt I

OLD HUNSTANTON

STOW BARDOLPH

had to paint. It is an area that is often photographed and painted, but I could not resist it either. With the lovely waving reed bed in the foreground and the mill looking straight out on to the marsh land, it was marvellous. The mill itself is now converted into a house, as most mills seem to be, but it still retains its striking architectural charm. With the gulls swirling on the sea breeze, it was a sight that summed up Norfolk for me. It is a fascinating and greatly underrated area.

Finally, in Norfolk, I was travelling along a country road and was enthralled by the sky. It was purplish and low down on the horizon – and there, yet again, was another windmill. The top was silhouetted clearly

CLEY

54

against that dark background and, in the sharp light, it dominated the cluster
of small cottages and buildings. It was typical of Norfolk, although without
the colour of the sky it wouldn't have been so interesting. However, I thought
it demanded a quick water-colour, so here is Burnham Overy Staithe.

BURNHAM OVERY

STAITHE

CASTLE COMBE

56

WILTSHIRE

During my first visit to Wiltshire, I visited Lacock with my old school friends. Close by is the famous Castle Combe, where *Dr Dolittle* was filmed. It is an incredible place — just right for a film set — and I had to paint a picture. There is so much that appeals: the texture of the stone, the peg-tile roofs, the bridge going through the centre of the village, the sweeping countryside and the woods on the hill. The whole thing is just ideal — so English. I can imagine what it must be like for people coming from abroad; our villages must have the same effect on them as Venice had on me when I visited Italy — totally different, yet totally absorbing and beautiful. Castle Combe made just such an impression on me — it is a wonderful place.

The thumbnail water-colour sketch shows the entrance to the village. I parked some way out, as the villagers do not like cars left all over the place; they dislike technological litter of any kind (they have even got rid of their television aerials). So you walk down through this entrance, into the richness of the village itself.

Wiltshire is a vast county and I could spend months just wandering and sketching. Often I head for an area that reminds me of a poet, a painter, a writer or whatever, just to see what influenced them. In Wiltshire I headed

for the village of Marten and Marten Down, which is a nature reserve. These were once the haunts of that great writer W. H. Hudson. He wrote *The Shepherd's Life*, among other things, which was based on that area of downland. What I saw there, which I thought was quite charming, was a track with a large hawthorn tree. Underneath the tree was a signpost saying 'Marten' – it looked particularly pleasing because it was made of local materials. All country milestones, gateposts and signposts should be made of traditional materials. An old gate, half open and covered with brambles, is so atmospheric – and there it was, a simple subject saying everything.

MARTEN

The village itself is almost faultless, a little bit over-gardened, but still with a lot of character. There was an old pump in the centre of the green, overlooked by thatched cottages. The scene reminded me so much of *The Shepherd's Life*. Way up on the downs was lovely too, and made even more memorable by the skylarks. I sat for about an hour and a half looking down on the village, just listening to the larks. As it is a nature reserve, the birds are safe to sing and rear their young. Seeing the downland and the traditional thatched cottages, and linking them with Hudson and Caleb, the shepherd, was just perfect.

CASTLE COM

MARTEN

61

DORSET

After Wiltshire I wandered on to Dorset. I know and love the county through Hardy, its links with shepherding and sheep, its wildlife, its landscapes and, of course, its villages. I have many friends there and it greatly appeals to me in all seasons of the year.

Through all my roaming around Dorset since the mid-1960s, the one village that has dominated my thoughts is Powerstock, which is where I used to stay in the local pub. The village is situated within the most beautiful combes, shallow valleys and green knolls, just about six miles inland of Bridport. I have been involved in painting, television programmes and radio in the area, because it is one of those places of endless enjoyment.

Powerstock village itself is most interesting, with a very early church. You can see a switchback landscape surrounding the village. If you observe natural history, birds, mammals, insects and flowers, you are never disappointed – and Powerstock is situated in the middle of an unspoilt landscape with its rich wildlife. When I first went to Dorset I was especially intrigued by its butterflies.

This water-colour shows the Three Horseshoes pub where I used to stay with my friends Pete and Stella Ford until they retired. They moved on to nearby Bridport, which is in south-west Dorset between Lyme Regis and

Dorchester. If you walk away from the pub, in the centre of Powerstock, you see typical Dorset cottages, some thatched, including an amazing one at an angle to the lane itself.

Powerstock is very special to me; the surrounding landscape, including Powerstock Forest and Eggardon Hill, is superb for all forms of wildlife. I did a film for the BBC called *Dorset Dream*, which was based on this area. It is not just a dream – fortunately, it is still also a reality.

O W E R S T O C K

Powerstock Mill is no longer working, but the farmer who owns it
intends to restore it soon. It has a lovely atmosphere and such romantic charm.
The original wheel of the mill was made in Bridport, and the farmer is going
to search out a craftsman to renovate it. There is a terrific quality about these
old water-mills, particularly when they are small and tucked away.

Here we have another sepia drawing of a village, called Burton
Bradstock, which is just on the edge of Bridport. I have to travel quite a
distance in a day, when researching my books. Consequently, when I come
across interesting or attractive places, I sketch them and make notes to store

POWERSTOCK

65

the mood and information for later use. This village, which I know quite well, is typical of Dorset, its thatched cottages have cobby stone walls, and there is some Georgian architecture in the centre. I thought it would be a nice idea just to sketch the slightly grander side of this village on the way to Bridport.

Not far from Bridport is Abbotsbury. As you come over the hill, it stretches before you in the valley. H. J. Massingham, in his book *Country Relics*, said: 'The last time I saw a shepherd with a crook was on the downs near Abbotsbury.' Still, it was good to see the sheep on the downs, even without a shepherd.

BURTON

BRADSTOCK

ABBOTSBURY

66

On the edge of Dorset, near the New Forest, I was visiting my aunt at Poole. On the way back I was thinking of subjects for the book, when I came across this wonderful post office. The 'office' was half a cottage. I suppose you walked up the garden path to send a parcel, buy a pound of tomatoes, and then have a cup of tea with the local postmaster. I thought it was so typical of Dorset.

I know there are many of these lovely post offices dotted around the countryside, but for how much longer will they survive? I wonder when regulations will suddenly say that they do not comply with some EU directive – that it is a crime to buy tomatoes and post a letter at the same time? It is vital that these small shops are kept open for the welfare of the inhabitants, as well as for the character of the village itself.

In addition, of course, not all villagers have cars, particularly the older ones, and so the local shop provides a much-needed service. Our baker here in Hertfordshire, John, not only delivers bread three times a week but also gets the coal in for the old people, does their shopping, gets their pensions and makes sure that they are all right. Conservation is about rural communities as well as landscape and wildlife. We want a thriving countryside where people live, work and care for each other. Every village needs its pub, church, school and shop to maintain its heart and soul.

EDMONDSHAM

70

THE NEW FOREST

From Dorset I wandered over the border to the edge of the New Forest. When you think of the New Forest you imagine trees, clearings and ponies grazing, but I was looking for its architecture, and I found two superb cottages. One was a straightforward Victorian cottage with a pony grazing nearby on the green. The other was a thatched cottage surrounded by woodlands. In my picture I have shown it late in the day. I looked over the hedge, which was similar to a flowering cherry – a wild bullace probably – and there was a light in the window. A wisp of smoke drifted out of the chimney, and a woman came out to look at the washing. I asked her if she minded me painting a picture of her cottage and we had a chat. I told her that in my opinion the cottage was just right: there was no patio along the front, she hadn't paved the path and she hadn't hidden the washing round the back. She said, 'You are not going to paint the washing?' 'Of course I am,' I replied, 'I don't want you to touch it – it's all part of the atmosphere.' She agreed and admitted that she was very proud of her washing.

For me, it was everything that a village cottage should be.

BRAMSHAW

SURREY

I found myself in Surrey during the summer because another butterfly reserve was being opened by Butterfly Conservation, and I had a wonderful opportunity to see the purple emperor – a magnificent creature.

While in the area, I decided to have a look at some of the local villages and architecture. I was soon rewarded, for, not far from Hascombe, at Dunsfold, I found a lovely farmhouse on the green, with barns attached, so I decided to do a sepia drawing. The combination of the large, dominating tree and the

73

old-style country architecture was irresistible. Then the apparently never-ending link with writers and artists of the past dawned on me again. Archibald Thorburn, the great painter of birds, lived at Hascombe, three miles from where I was doing the sketch. So I headed for Hascombe.

It is a sign of the times that nobody in the local pub had heard of Thorburn or knew where he had lived. Fortunately, the rector was a better bet, and soon I was standing outside the house. Thorburn built the place in 1903 on thirteen acres of ground, and it has hardly altered since. Only a handful of people have owned it and the present owner invited Betty and me in. She couldn't have been more helpful: she showed us round the house and the garden, and then the small outside studio. I was very excited by the studio, as it is almost identical to the one I work in at Water End. I built mine not to copy Thorburn but to be in sympathy with the rest of my cottage – yet we both had a peg-tile roof and tarred, boarded walls. This was where Thorburn had once sat and encouraged small mammals and birds to come in through the window so that he could sketch from life. I couldn't believe that I was actually standing in the place where the great man had lived and worked. It was the same feeling that I had had when I first went to the birthplace of Thomas Hardy at Higher Bockhampton and then on to Max Gate, the house that he later built in Dorchester. The studio had the same atmosphere – I tried to catch it on this study sheet.

I am a huge admirer of Thorburn's art and, inevitably I suppose, it has been an influence in my work, particularly in the early days, when I was observing wildlife and trying to see things in terms of paintings. Since those days, my interests and passions have taken me beyond birds, but I still love watching them

and painting them – hence the mistle thrush in this book. Thorburn was one of our greatest natural history painters; the charm of his work lay in his ability to observe living things in their natural habitat and capture their essence. He was more than a painter – he was a craftsman. He had tremendous skill in applying paint to paper, but he was also a master of composition.

HASCOMBE

This painting represents many of the villages visited in my journeys. When I started this book earlier on in the year, in almost every village I was delighted to hear the song of the mistle thrush, or 'storm cock' as it is called – a wonderful description. Sometimes I was caught in torrential rain, high winds and cold weather. But there always seemed to be a mistle thrush about, and so I had to paint one – it is one of my favourite birds. It heralds the spring, like the first butterfly, like the swallow, like the rooks in March. The mistle thrush is the first to sing out and say: 'Yes, we have got a new year coming along.'

As I was travelling through Surrey thinking about villages and architecture, I was brought up with a jolt when I saw a Dorking cockerel, close to Dorking – fascinating. I do love chickens and cockerels, and Dorkings are most attractive. There he was showing himself off on a fence post, surrounded by wild roses. It was almost too good to be true. I decided I had to paint a cockerel and it was perfect that it should be a Dorking.

Just as I had painted the village cockerel, so I decided to paint the village cat. Travelling around villages, you usually see domestic animals, and you don't go far before you see a cat, either on a roof, in a garden, on a gatepost or looking out of a window. This huge ginger tom with a geranium in a pot behind him is typical. The window is open and there is a bit of lace curtain slightly blowing out. The cat is standing on the window ledge with his tail up between the flower-heads of the geranium. I am very fond of large ginger tom-cats. I have two and I love their colour, which reminds me of a fox, and the way they behave like small tigers. Sadly, they can also be destructive, and the secret is to keep them very well fed so they do not start

wandering and stalking the local wildlife. I have to admit, now, that this cat is one of ours. He is special, having disappeared and come back almost dead with a snare caught tight around his body. He was totally wild, but we fed

him up and it took three years to get him right. Now he won't go outside unless I pick him up and put him out. I don't like to see cats killing wild birds, but a collar with a bell can get caught on things. So keep them really well fed and they should have no energy or desire to chase birds.

SUSSEX

One of my most enjoyable journeys was back to Sussex. I have been visiting the county for years. The first time I went there was in 1940, as a little boy, for about two weeks during the Battle of Britain. The country-side made a tremendous impact on me and I can still remember the beautiful, green, rolling downland. Later on, my interest in shepherding took

AMBERLEY

80

me back to the county many times – indeed, one day, I would love to do a book on shepherds and shepherding. Amberley is one of the many villages I return to: it is an outstanding place with wonderful early architecture – typical Sussex houses with half-timber frames. I remember going into the village pub and seeing an exceptional collection of sheep bells hanging from the beams. I could have chosen many places in Sussex, but I decided on Amberley as it is so outstanding of its type.

AMBERLEY

Gordon Benningfield

NORTHAMPTONSHIRE

Last February I found myself at Yardley Hastings. It was very cold, but that didn't stop me enjoying the village and its lovely architecture. This picture struck me immediately – the simple church tower, the lych-gate to the right of the pollarded spiky tree and the cottages end-on to me – an interesting combination of architecture typical of an English village centre. I thought this fairly detailed pencil drawing was sufficient without any colour. It is so important to the character and charm of these old village centres that new buildings, new shops and street lights are kept away. The traditional heart of a village should stay as it was meant to be – uncluttered by the flotsam and jetsam of the late twentieth century.

YARDLEY

HASTINGS

SUFFOLK

Sadly, time allowed only one visit to Suffolk, which is a shame as it is a marvellous county. Approaching Kersey, you see the church before the village. By the cottages there is a pump with a seat beside it, and down in the village you find timber-framed houses and a few shops. At the bottom, in the centre, a tributary of the River Brett splashes over the road. The substantial church dominates the scene. It was the combination of the multi-coloured roofs, some with red tiles and some covered in lichen, and the overhanging gables that inspired me to do this picture.

KERSEY

Gordon Beningfield

KENT

In Kent I wanted to find oast-houses which were still in use. They have become a real part of the Kent landscape. I did see one or two buildings, but they had all been converted into homes. Eventually, I came across a group

of oast-houses in a tiny valley surrounded by apple blossom. Oast-houses and apple blossom are a traditional Kent combination. Again, thinking about writers and painters, it was a scene dear to Roland Hilder, who made the Kent landscape so famous through his art. It was marvellous to see so many young apple trees – it was appropriate too, as it was near Faversham and Brogdale. Brogdale is the home of that wonderful collection of traditional fruit trees saved by the Prince of Wales. It has about 2,000 apple trees, with varieties dating back to Roman times, as well as 2,000 other soft fruits.

I returned to Kent in the autumn to see the fruit after it had grown from blossom to apples – the idea appealed to me. Once there I wanted to paint a picture, not produce an illustration of apples on a branch, so I used my old apple basket: I piled up some of the bright-red varieties, which are inviting and attractive, and stood the basket by the side of a tree. It seemed to sum up the charm and the wonder of our traditional apples. Apart from being good to eat, apples are delightful to look at. Above all, these are English apples, which I believe are the best in the world. It is encouraging to see so many types, and I hope that the salvation and promotion of these valuable trees will be successful. I can't understand why people eat French apples, or why supermarkets stock them. Our apples are unique, but producers have nevertheless been encouraged to grub up their orchards. It's a shame – there is simply no comparison between a French apple and an English apple.

By coincidence, just before I finished this book, a friend informed me that her cousin still has a traditional oast-house on the farm she shares with her husband. It was wonderful – the appearance and the lingering smell of the hops was well worth the late visit, and so I painted it.

LITTLEBOURNE

YORKSHIRE

I don't go to Yorkshire often, but whenever I do it always appeals to me. This beautiful wood, near the village of Masham, is owned by the Woodland Trust. The charm of it, for me, lies in this sparkling little stream bouncing over stones and pebbles. I painted it in autumn, although I would like to paint it again in the middle of summer. I love the autumn in woodland because you can hear acorns dropping and small birds twittering and rummaging around the roots of the trees. Amongst the undergrowth there were lots of wood pigeons. I do like everyday things, and this was so attractive that I couldn't resist it. I would love to go back to Yorkshire more often; it is so impressive.